DEDICATION

THIS BOOK IS DEDICATED TO THE WISDOM FROM WHENCE IT CAME.

ALL PRAISE IS DUE TO ALLAH (GOD)

Acknowledgments

As-Salaam Alaikum (Peace Be Unto You)

I am a laborer at the Final Call Administration Building located in Chicago, Illinois.

My wife of forty-four years, Sister Katie M. Muhammad, my daughter Shakeelah Muhammad, my two son's Arthur and Jabril have also accepted this mission of The Mental Resurrection of The Mentally Dead.

I thank Allah for the teachings of The Honorable Elijah Muhammad and His National and International representative Minister Louis Farrakhan. It is this truth that inspired this book.

I truly love my wife, my family and The Nation Of Islam.

All Praise Is Due To Allah

Arthur Muhammad

In The Name Of Allah The Beneficent The Merciful

First and foremost, I thank Almighty God Allah for blessing me with my mother and father, who proved that they loved me and my siblings beyond a shadow of a doubt. About twenty years ago, I mentioned to my mother, "I didn't realize until recently that we were poor." Then she said, "Boy, I would stretch a dollar until George Washington smiled." I said to myself- Damn! My father would say to us, "What a wise man can do with $1,000.00 a fool can't do with $10,000.00." My father could not tolerate nobody who was foolish with money.

My mother and father loved singing. The whole family sang in our church choir. When I was a freshman in high school, I wanted to join The Wendell Phillips A cappella choir. I was asked by the director to join, that was 1970. I found out about twenty years later that you could not join that choir when you were a freshman, and check this out- The choir had an invitation to a music festival that

4

was in Europe-Beirut, Germany! There were over sixty members in the choir and only twenty-two members could go. I was one of the members chosen to go. I was elated when after one of the practices, the director asked me, "Do you think your mother would like to go as a chaperone." I stood there shocked. Then he asked me again, calling my name. "Arthur, do you think your mother would like to go to Germany as a chaperone?" I said, "I'll go and ask her." He said, "Let me know next week and we can meet." I left school at that moment and went home missing classes. I was so excited, and my mother got to go also.

If my father were a teenager in this time we're living in, he probably would be one of THE BADDEST rappers. He really had a way with words. He constantly quoted scriptures and poems to us. It was when Muhammad University opened (M.U.I.) that my wife enrolled my oldest son. He needed a poem for Mother's Day and he asked his mother to help him with the poem. She told him to ask me. God is my witness, this is when I found out that Allah had blessed me to write poems.

There are over 800,000 words in the English language and we make decisions based on the information and education we have.

I thank Allah (God) for the Life-Giving Teachings of The Most Honorable Elijah Muhammad and his National and International Representative Minister Louis Farrakhan.

This book of poems is by Allah (God's) permission "MY TESTIMONY" which is also the first poem and the title of this book.

I thank Allah for Brother Timothy and his wife Sister LeShaundra. I have a gift to write that is a spark. My brother poured gasoline on the spark and they took it to another level. All Praise Is due to Allah.

"…our Unity will solve 95% of our problems." -The Honorable Elijah Muhammad

MY TESTIMONY- By Arthur Muhammad

MY TESTIMONY

Inspired by Allah

The year was 1986. The month was September.

These words that I heard I pray I'll always remember.

There is nothing more valuable than divine spoken words.

I'm constantly being blessed from these words that I heard.

Here's the well-developed thought that got my attention.

This wisdom, knowledge and understanding caused me to listen.

The words I heard hooked me, fished me, out of this world's water.

The Man who spoke these words became my spiritual Father.

I must have listened to this lecture ten (10) times in three days.

This wisdom changed my life my conscious was raised.

This Man has an understanding only the best knower can give.

That has affected millions helped changed the way we live.

He can't be nailed to the cross by Allah's grace; He's alive.

He's been doing what He's doing since 1955.

He's surrounded by the enemy but THE FORCE holds them back.

He continues working-proving Elijah Muhammad is right and exact.

We must continue to work laying this divine foundation.

Our fate will be sealed losing another generation.

This is the foundation of every righteous civilization.

The Nation of Islam is blessed with the right information.

The root knowledge of Elijah Muhammad is divinely complete.

The enemy knows when firmly rooted, will make their world obsolete.

THE FIRST LAW: WORSHIP NO GOD
BUT ALLAH is the lecture I heard.

Farrakhan is blessed to speak divine well-
constructed words.

Who Are They?

They were allowed to rule with one book of math

60,000 minus 1 are in the straight path

Everything They touch They alter, They leave nothing straight

The education They gave us more than likely is fake

They took us from our land their names to us They gave

They became our masters we became their slaves

They have thoroughly deceived us and They taught us well

How to facilitate this wickedness now this world's a living hell

The truth we won't accept the enemy remains the teacher

The worst of those among us are the pastors and the preachers

They have made them shepherds and we've been led to the slaughter

In desperate need of good shepherds to save our sons and daughters

Out of ALLAH, Gods mercy you had a chance to Atone

But after 6,000 years won't leave the righteous alone

And all those years They have been their own manager

They did what they did because They didn't have a challenger

They know the prophecy(truth) and the Time but won't surrender

Now it's Time that They meet ALLAH'S #1 contender

He's solid as a rock stands on the strongest foundation

You can read of this champion in the book of revelations

He's of the true vine organized not messy

He drilled down and connected into the root of Jesse

Those roots go deep, He saw the sacrificial lamb

His soul has been rocked in the bosom of Abraham

He knows and said with out doubt, before Abraham was I AM

A new star has been created transmitting a new light

He's not taking no prisoners has Satan's devils in flight

They were made an offer but they wouldn't retire

It's too late now The Time Has Expired

They exceeded the limit They went down to the wire

They didn't realize They were playing with Fire

Now confused and perplexed we can hear the wicked scream

They (fools) tried to put the fire out using gasoline

Now they are being chased running out of Zion

They were warned of the day the Lamb would turn into a Lion

It's The Shock of the Hour, the deceivers are surprised

The Lamb that turned into a Lion won't make a deal or compromise

We have decided to give you and your hommies a shovel

Because the life you've been living is on the lowest level

Even now as we speak
you're digging your own
grave

Told you the truth and you
won't behave

You had many chances to
turn your life around

Evidence of you doing it
cannot be found

We've watched you for
many days and hours

How you stalked and infected whoever
you could devour

You are an international
criminal the whole world
you've infected

Your resume to Allah's
kingdom has been rejected

Now all doors are closed there's
nowhere to go

That's the way it is we reap what we
sow

The Time has come, We have to hand down this sentence

90% of the time you've shown no repentance

You did your evil with strength and endurance

ALLAH is pulling your plug no one else you'll influence

You have to admit you did this to yourself

THE FINAL CALL has been given JUSTICE OR ELSE

The Shock of the Hour

He came to take care of serious business

A promise made to Abraham in the Bible's Genesis

He's come to Judge, Has the Ultimate Power

The Qur'an calls this time The Shock of the Hour

Allah told Satan not to take His servants life

It's constantly done someone has to pay the price

The Saviour came to America with the remedy

To rescue His people from a vicious enemy

He came to do what many could not conceive or try

He came prepared to climb a mountain (40) miles high

Had to raise one from among us who's heart was pure

Who would accept the responsibility with His Divine Cure

The first time Elijah met Him, He passed a crucial test

Recognized the Saviour though He came in sinful flesh

When The Saviour arrived, we were in a hell of a dilemma

But Elijah was receptive raised His spiritual antennas

Elijah became The Saviours one hundred percent convert

Walking His post in a perfect manner keeping always on the alert

Has a divine recipe with all the right ingredients

But can only be used by one who's totally obedient

Satan tried to make Him think His mission wasn't relevant

A Judge told Him it's like trying to put pants on a elephant

Tried to make His faith to be flimsy as cooked spaghetti

But He boldly told the Judge, I got one leg in already

The Messenger worked hard to save us, from Allah's wrath

Overcame all obstacles that got in His path

All Praises be to Allah, another Atom was cracked

Farrakhan is a witness, Elijah is right and exact

Who and what is a sign of the Apostles victory

The resurrection of the Nation made modern day history

Through Farrakhan the mission can be completed

Satan's Influence in our Brother has been deleted

We have been found, it's of Divine
you can hear it

Submission is the master of the self-
accusing spirit

This has proven to be our number
one problem

Entire submission masters and
increases the volume

Self-improvement, self-correction
puts everybody in check

Because this wisdom got lost the
whole world has been wrecked

We are the golden vessels, to the
God more precious than pearls

Though we looked as if slain from
the foundation of the world

We can beat the prophecy though
the time is critical

Farrakhan is proof that we are of the
right material

What is the thorough knowledge we
need to understand

The self-accusing spirit is a divine reprimand

God's nature within us the Creators gift to us all

The truth ends the confusion…This is the Final Call.

WHO IS THIS PERSON

He was in existence before anybody else

He's the absolute Master of improving Himself

This may be new to you but not complicated

There is none like Him He's self-created

He started alone has no Father or Mother

All by Himself no sister or brother

He's the Power in the darkness before there was light

He's the first to solve problems and make things right

He started time He created motion

He's the cause and the reason water is in the Ocean

There's no life without water He existed before that

He is Supreme Wisdom always right and exact

This is The Greatest story that can ever be told

This Person is talked about by all the Prophets new and old

The Sun is His symbol He's not a reflection

He is light unto Himself who causes chain reactions

There's not a person living or dead who did not benefit from His Knowledge

It's because of His Wisdom we have Universities and College

His truth was revealed when He eliminated darkness

You and I were created after His image and likeness

We are from Him this is our personality

Self-Improvement is the Wisdom to make it reality

Self-Examination Self-Analysis then Self-Correction

This vision we must use to produce our Resurrection

BEHOLD this person can make all things New

If you want to see this person search deep inside it's You.

Satan's Ways and Thinking

When you speak prematurely without actual facts

And what you say is not accurate not right and exact

It seems every time you speak you cunningly find fault

Now the words you speak are taken with a grain of salt

This kind of activity makes anyone suspicious

A liars words are not spiritually nutritious

Do you do this unaware, is your mind gone

Have you been left in your inordinacy blindly wandering on

Are you involved in criminal activities hoping no one knows

Doing favors for the enemies for fear of being exposed

Don't never forget Satan is wickedly wise

His/her ability to act righteous is his biggest disguise

Knows all the rituals and procedures and charity he pays but

Can you fool a Muslim? Not nowadays

Satan makes us think we're something we're not

He'll make you think He's giving you something you've already got

Don't forget why the Minister took away the titles

These principles can be found in our Quran and Bibles

Is your mind clear or is your vision fogged

Do you lean toward your own understanding and can't stand dialogue

Are you a tyrant and care not for those who think

Envious of others light and their light try to shrink

Has the ways of Satan's world slithered into our Nation

Is there five percent among us causing major complications

Time is running out we need to change in a hurry

Our constant rebellion proves that we're not worthy

Woe to all the wicked shepherds you are the minority

Allah is going to get you for misusing your authority

Even if our lives have been dark and murky

Allah's prime attributes are…Beneficence and Mercy

If we atone and mean it in our hearts

Allah can wash away sin and give us a new start

HYPOCRITES AND AGENTS

Hypocrites and agents rolling up their sleeves

Ready to carry out their plans when the Minister leaves

Analyze what's going on while The Minister is among us

What do you think will happen when Allah takes him from us

The enemy can't be successful with our original instructions

They'll try to make the Believer doubt, and cause interruption

So many brothers and sisters look good to the eyes

Suits, bowties, and garments may be a disguise

Masters of deception know how to stay out of sight

Satan keeps himself hidden but his laborers are in the light

We were born in this day and time to settle an old score

The time and what must be done we must wage war

Against Satan, the deceivers, the maker of devils

They have deceived the whole world on multiple levels

There's an exalted assembly Satan can't manipulate

The divine force stays around them Satan can no way penetrate

Be careful how you react when things don't go your way

Seek refuge in Allah be patient, fast and pray

Are you constantly doing things, which cause trouble and division

What principles and standards do you use to make decisions

Mixed feelings and controversies are in full effect

How we handle them is key don't do something you'll regret

IMAGINE

Imagine a doctor who doesn't write prescriptions

Imagine the newspaper industry not getting subscriptions

Imagine going to school where there are no scholars

Imagine little boys growing up without their fathers

Imagine photographers who don't take pictures

Imagine a preacher who doesn't study scriptures

Imagine shepherds who go to sleep with the sheep

Imagine someone who can't swim diving in the deep

Imagine an object flying a half mile by a half mile

Imagine tuning up on people's thoughts without turning a dial

Imagine putting clothes in the cleaners that aren't dirty

Imagine teaching the Whiteman is the devil in the 1930's

Imagine all the people who graduated from college

Imagine all of them together to solve our problems have not the knowledge

Imagine what would happen when men really start respecting women

Imagine the end of this world and the start of a new beginning

Imagine the men working together to change her environment

Imagine the men working together to put the old one in retirement

Imagine a world of freedom, justice and equality

Imagine the Master of the day of judgement getting rid of this society

THE SOLUTION

We have witnessed mischief being perfected

We witnessed children growing up unprotected

We are witnessing shepherds leading people to destruction

Witnessing in the highest places all kinds of corruption

Pedophile Priest who are not arrested

Obvious crimes at the top that are not contested

One error after another constantly repeated

Our economic system is about to be deleted

An educational system dumbing people down

Men who would teach the truth No Where to be found

Millions have gone to school Millions graduated from College

Billions all over suffering from the lack of knowledge

Who's been teaching the people what have we been taught

We need a new teaching that will spark new thought

Who has the solution to these multitude of problems

Where is the Supreme Wisdom that will ultimately solve them

Everywhere we look we can see the victims

Who have been intoxicated in this satanic system

Its purposely done these acts of evil are malicious

Ignorance is the enemy and it's getting ridiculous

The solution is here Farrakhan makes it clearer

All of us can solve the problem if we look in the mirror

Each and everyone of us represent a problem

Humility and honesty will help to solve them

Follow Allah's instruction He will give you the remedy

He'll prepare a table for you in the presence of the enemy

A LIGHT UNTO HIMSELF

ALLAH is a light unto Himself He put Himself in motion

He gives everything aim and purpose He put the water in the ocean

This fact must be mentioned there's no life without water

We're talking about the best knower who is the Original Man's Father

There is none like HIM HE has no associates

Comparing HIM to anyone will not be appropriate

This is Supreme Wisdom awesome more than remarkable

When ALLAH created Himself from nothing HE destroyed the impossible

This was a one-time occurrence a divine phenomenon

Approximately 78 trillion years ago definitely not common

ALLAH'S wisdom is perpetual and never ending

What we're talking about is just the beginning

ALLAH studied Himself the only one (1) in existence

There was no one to oppose Him there was no resistance

THE VISION (my grandson)

I see him for this world having no desire

I pray ALLAH through my daughter puts out that fire

I see his Father standing firm, working hard for our Nation

I see their life an example and cause for celebration

I hear him at an early age, reciting the actual facts

I see him striving always to be right and exact

I see him running marathons at 400 years old

I see the Wisdom of GOD taking root deep down in his soul

I see him living The Restrictive Law and being successful

I see him qualified a true and righteous vessel

I see him constantly exposed to a righteous environment

I see a Soldier of Farrakhan putting the old one in retirement

I see the M.G.T. and Vanguard protecting all our little lambs

Oh, ALLAH make us successful as thou did Muhammad and Abraham

I see him learning lessons only ALLAH can teach

I see him doing things that others only preach

I see his Grand Mother, my wife she's like a glove

She has him covered always with the Spirit of Love

I see him eating the way Elijah Muhammad prescribed

I see his work being what the Holy Quran describes

I see his Uncles of M.U.I persecuted, for helping make him new

I see my Grandson, their Nephew,
coming to the rescue

The Oscars

(And The Best Actor Is)?

Satan wrote the script the whole
World is the stage

All the 85% have been given a page

In classrooms teaching without
actual facts

The teachers don't realize they're
just putting on an act

The gym rooms are where the
students practice their stunts

Satan's religious institutions turn
good men into monks

The same people who produce and
manufacture guns

Are those who certify the Priest and
qualify the Nuns

John Deer and Caterpillar make the
best tractors

Harvard, Yale and Princeton
produce the best Actors

This is War and its going on in Heaven

All strategic organizations have a 007

The time is serious this is the final chapter

The President is being nominated for the best Actor

This had to happen the previous actors were a bore

This has never happened at the Academy Awards before

Reagan was an actor, Clinton was a joke

Bush with his foolishness made the whole world choke

We're praying for Obama hope he gets out the trap

Brother toss all that garbage that's been placed in your lap

Now let's take a look into the religious societies

This is the category with all the varieties

When witnessing these characters we need divine protection

This is the category of special effects and deception

Have you considered what's been taught or what we've been believing

These actors are masters of making evil fair seeming

Let's see: We have wolves in sheep's clothing; we have scholars acting wise

We have out right devils who have outgrown their disguise

Never before has a group like this been seen

But everyday in Satan's world is like Halloween

The sheep have been abandoned, the Shepherds have gone to sleep

Always making promises they don't intend to keep

Body builders using steroids to produce muscles

Preachers talking God but it's just a hustle

The Rabbis, the Imams and the Pastor

Follow Satan's script now this world's a disaster

Don't forget this is the Academy Awards

It looks like a Benz but its actually a Ford

Satan's devils can see Farrakhan marching up to Zion

Every step of the way hear Him roaring like a Lion

The Script said left Farrakhan went Right

The script said get down; Farrakhan took flight

Farrakhan is The One He has the Script from ALLAH'S LAMB

He got it following the footsteps of Muhammad and Abraham

Satan had Louis Walcott at one time on their roster

Louis Farrakhan will never be nominated for an Oscar

Judas, Lucifer, Beelzebub and Baal; Allah has already warned you

He's sending you all to HELL

These Brothers and Sisters are smooth, some of the best ice skaters

Envious and jealous looking good but are haters

Farrakhan the divine strategist and the ultimate soldier

Keeps His friends close and His enemies closer

Unfortunately we have many great pretenders

And many; of them are around the Minister

Farrakhan is the house of God, He is the Kabah

Standing fearless and strong seeking refuge in Allah

Prophecy Fulfilled

He was willed into existence by the self-created One (1)

The Wisdom That He uses is second to none.

He's The First Person since the Creator to Master The Universe

What He teaches Elijah Muhammad can never be reversed.

In a Descendant of a slave Supreme Wisdom was activated

Mathematics is Islam this was divinely calculated.

Supreme Wisdom is the best of all Ideologies

Supreme Wisdom will produce Freedom, Justice and Equality.

Supreme Wisdom the use of Knowledge to make our lives complete

Supreme Wisdom will eventually make all others obsolete.

The reality of God is no longer a mystery

Prophecy has been fulfilled the start of new history.

The wickedly wise were looking for the birth of the Messiah

Who would have ever thought it was the Georgia born Elijah.

Prophets spoke of Him before His birth

He's worth more than all the gold in the Earth.

All written of Him, He Will Fulfill

His only desire is to do Allah (God's) Will.

The work He does causes the evil to tremble

The very likeness of God He so closely resembles.

Satan's world is rapidly coming to a close

The teachings of Elijah leaves Satan totally exposed.

He's the Wisest Man we have ever met

He teaches us to be the cause that produces the Effect.

By Allah Himself He's divinely educated

And the Wisdom of this world He totally dominated.

Satan thinks they can hurt Him with their slander and lies

They infiltrate our Nation with stool pigeons and spies.

The truth (He Farrakhan) speaks puts troubled minds at ease

This truth is now affecting our brothers and sisters overseas.

Farrakhan a free man went on three (3) world tours

Our Brother Traveling International makes the wicked insecure.

Fearless and teaches wisdom millions have never heard

He is a man of God and does not speak idle words.

A.D.L. and J.D.L. in a hell of a situation

Trying to handle The Messiah with a sixth (6th) grade education.

Then they fired on our Brother and Farrakhan fired right back

Standing upright and ready for another attack.

When the smoke cleared Farrakhan's eyes were wide open

It was a blistering attack but no signs of Him choking.

The F.O.I. and M.G.T. held their post and survived

Trained well made fearless what's general order #5.

Stand down Satan this Louis is not
Joe

And what He's capable of you really
don't want to know.

By Allah (God's) permission He's
been unstoppable

Doing what most people thought
was mission impossible.

Allah alone He serves and that
Satan can't handle

Melts down their assaults like a
flame on a candle.

Satan thought-just another Black
man they were gonna devour

But they greatly miscalculated
Master Fard Muhammad's power.

And Elijah Muhammad to Satan is
nothing nice

They did all they could to stop Him
they miscalculated twice.

Today with Farrakhan the wicked
are in another bout

It's your third miscalculation-strike three (3) and you're out!

From the Author

I was born July 6, 1954 in Cook County Hospital Chicago, Il. My father-Theodore Thomas was born in Arkansas. My mother-Lucinda, affectionately known as Sue by all of her friends and associates, was born in Alabama.

I grew up on the low-end 39th street Chicago. The low-end is what people back in the day called that area. My mother was a housewife and the whippings I got as a child are probably why I'm alive today. Thank Almighty God for all mothers. My father was a door-to-door salesman. He sold Fuller Products. Not the Fuller brush, but Fuller Products as a BLACKMAN. My father would say, "Go door-to-door, floor-to-floor and let the people do their shopping in the living-room." This was in the 50's when I was a baby.

Imagine a BLACKMAN with a wife and four children living in a basement apartment with two rooms and a kitchen, being audited by the IRS and having to pay back taxes. He revealed this to me before he passed away and showed me all the receipts of the payments. That pissed me totally off.

We moved out of the basement two blocks away into a three-bedroom apartment in the early 60's. It was about three years later, there was a fire and we lost everything.   I thank Almighty God for my father and my mother because they did not unravel. Thank God. My father, about a year and a half later, bought the house in which we once lived in the basement of. "Faith without works is dead."

Thank you – Brother Arthur Muhammad

ABOUT THE COVER

The cover of this book was photographed by Brother Arthur Muhammad.

It was early in the morning at sunrise. What you see is the sun with the moon reflecting it's light in the distance.

Just another one of our brother's gifts.

www.ingramcontent.com/pod-product-compliance
Lightning Source LLC
Chambersburg PA
CBHW030526220526
45463CB00007B/2732